S0-BPO-212

SOUTH OF CONTRARY

Larry Christianson

South of Contrary

Larry
Christianson

NORTH STAR PRESS OF ST. CLOUD, INC.

St. Cloud, Minnesota

Dedicated
to
Oliver Hodgson of Bluefields, Nicaragua—
very special and longtime *hakunna matata* friend
on mellow edges south of contrary

Cover Photo: Tom Plihal
Author Photo: Norma Christianson

Copyright © 2009 Larry Christianson

All rights reserved

First edition, May 2009

ISBN: 0-87839-337-4
ISBN-13: 978-0-87839-3337-4

Printed in the United States of America

Published by:
North Star Press of St. Cloud, Inc.
P.O. Box 451
St. Cloud, Minnesota 56302

www.northstarpress.com

List of Illustrations

CONTENTS

SOUTH OF CONTRARY

SOUTH OF CONTRARY

Still
Small voice
     of solitude,
     of silence.

Whispering through breezes
     soothing,
     settling quietly,
          calmly.

South of contrary—
     all along tattered
     ledges
     on inner landscapes
          of humanity.

Places of heart
     and spirit soaring
     on joyful journeys
          of hope.

Quirky landmarks
     and treasured milestones
     for all restless
          wanderers.
On mellow edges
     south of contrary.

—July 2008 while at Lake Three in the Boundary Waters awaiting the book release of *North of the Tension Line*

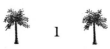

1

DOWN
SOUTH
DEFLECTIONS

DOWN SOUTH DEFLECTIONS

Down South deflections—
Perking up through the years
     scattered into quirky patterns
     near to heart and far away.
Spaces and places.
Beyond and beneath
     compass point—S.
Marking new pathways
     and old escapades,
     and deep yearnings of the spirit.

Down South—
A common metaphor
     transforming compass
          and charts.
A warm place
     inspiring calm hearts
          and curious minds.
A varied space as vast
     as the longings
          of humanity.

Down South—
     a cherished retreat
     of precise definition
          or vague location.
For meaningful memories
     along quiet roadways
          of relaxation.
For shifting gears
     on treasured journeys
     of personal renewal.
Beneath and beyond geography—
     deflections in all directions
          south.

—October 2008, as a companion to "Up North Reflections"

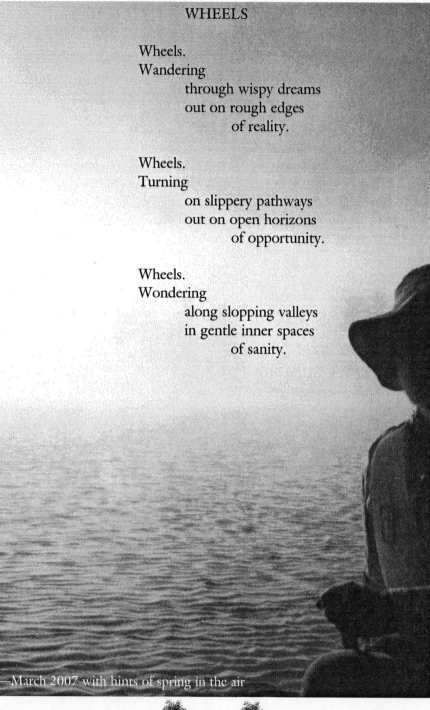

WHEELS

Wheels.
Wandering
    through wispy dreams
    out on rough edges
        of reality.

Wheels.
Turning
    on slippery pathways
    out on open horizons
        of opportunity.

Wheels.
Wondering
    along slopping valleys
    in gentle inner spaces
        of sanity.

—March 2007 with hints of spring in the air

PEACHY ALMOND

And the trivia board
      spun out a question
      of goofy intrigue:
           what nut is a member
           of the peach family?

Almond—
      who could have guessed!

Peachy almond—
      sounds like a new flavor
           of ice cream,
           of gourmet jam
               or specialty coffee.
Rather than a relationship!

Almond—
      a nut sharing the old family tree
           with juicy peaches,
      a nutty crossover,
      a fruity nutritional
           oddity.
An interesting question
      worthy of speculation
      on other agronomy
           connections.

Like my abiding passion
      for figs and olives—
      likely relatives happy
           in the long history
               of health food.

—May 2007 from the daily trivia question at the Mocha Monkey Coffee Shop

ZORRO

Zorro—
Arriving new
   in eras
   of struggle
      and oppression.

Dashing freedom fighter
   of expanding minds
      and lifting spirits,
   of rising hopes
      and generous hearts.
Slashing swords
   of gleaming silver
      and black.
Concealing mask
   of identity,
   not purpose.
Riding on a swift horse
   of galloping history,
   tortured and chock full
      of injustice.

Zorro—
Departing always
   in epochs
   of peace
      and justice.

For all!

—May 2005 for Norma—a dashing freedom adventurer of mind and spirit

SPRINGTIME

Superior
Springtime
    slowly coming.

Arriving with hints
    hesitant,
    sparse,
        and fleeting.

Blowing on a breeze
    softly,
    quietly,
        and freeing.

Melting ice hidden
    deeply,
    in hollows
        and rock piles.

Thawing the land
    and water,
    and winter
        weariness.

—April 2007 while at Cove Point Lodge at Beaver Bay along Lake Superior

LUNCH IN THE PARK

Restless riders
   rolling on asphalt
            anxiety.

Past flowers blooming
   in early autumn
            colors unfolding
            gently.

Against a hardly calm
   backdrop
            of trucks roaring
            and cars scurrying.

In a hurry.

A loud lunch
   in downtown park
   with boundary waters
            serenity scene.

Awaiting soon.

Playing a peaceful tune
   in my mind
            and heart.

—September 2008 eating outside in downtown Chaska on the day before heading north to the boundary waters

NIGHT WIND

Night wind.
Rising on restless
      strains
      of natural music.

Playing aloft in pines
      swaying,
      sawing away,
      shattering silences
          of wilderness evening.

Fading on night wind.

Running on reckless
      waters
      of rugged freedom.
Moving swiftly in waves
      lapping,
      rolling on,
      crashing shorelines
          of wilderness morning.

Arriving in stormy day.

—September 2008 while camping at Lake Four on a windy night in the wilderness country

11

COFFEE CULTURE

In countless coffee shops.
In community gathering
    places—

Where regular people feel special
    and special people
        feel regular.

Where care of hearts
    is the heart
        of care.
Where different kinds
    of happiness
        are encouraged.

Where real definitions
    of relaxation
        are expansive
        and inclusive.

And affirmed.
And accepted.

—September 2007 for theme poem for a reading at the Mocha Monkey in Waconia

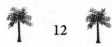

12

ON MAINTAINING

Low maintenance
    life—

Style of simplicity,
    sincerity,
    serenity.
Maybe even sanity.

Not enough cash
    to count nor stash,
    to guard nor worry about.
Nor fret over
    and labor under.
Burdens too heavy
    to bear.

Not enough cares to surmount
    nor surrender
    a hard-to-come-by
        gift of sanity.

High-maintenance
    heart.

—March 2006 even before a new opportunity appeared on the job horizon

MOCHA MONKEY

Mocha Monkey—
Fine coffees and teas
  from tropical places
    exotic,
    fertile,
    organic.
In sunshine zones
  all the planet
    round.

Mocha Monkey—
In a small town
  in north country
    Minnesota.
Full-bodied flavor.
Rich in texture.
Howling for humor and hope
  in a painful search
  for environmental
    integrity.
Relaxing refuge
  in a wounded
  and weary world.

Mocha Monkey—
Fair-trade haven
  in a hectic
  and harried time
    in history.
Pottery.
Hand crafted
  in earthy patterns
    beautiful,
    soothing.
Velvet soul!

—March 2007 for Pam and Mark, and coffee shop friends at the most relaxing place in town

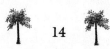

BEYOND

BOUNDARIES

WRITING ON WALLS

Writing on walls—
    in long forgotten
    out of the way
        places.

Along back roads.
And seaside towns
    sleepy in tropical
        rhythms.

In Puerto Limon—
    people of many colors
    painted on the run,
        shackled feet free
        on a once stark
            concrete wall.

Along the sea.
A mural of peace
    with a compelling message
        for the ages:
"the real enslavement
    of the people
    is ignorance."

—April 2008 twenty years after first being there in Costa Rica

LEAVING THE AMERICAN SECTOR

Checkpoint Charley welcome:
    "You are now leaving
        the American sector."

In multiple languages
    and complex nuances,
    guarding the doorway
        of Victor's 1959 Café.
Revolutionary Cuban cooking
    and Caribbean ambiance,
    more than authentic
        on the funky left-wing edge
        of leaving the American sector.

Scene changing,
    revolving through expressions
    of personal endearment
        and political sentiment
        written on wooden walls
            and plyboard ceilings.

Taking over—graffiti style!

Revolutionary conversation
    in the presence of Fidel:
        no problema,
        no mas guerra,
        no mas Bush!

Out of embargos crippling reach
    with soulful Latin jazz
    soothing the weary souls
        of all who dare
        to eat with the enemy.

—July 2006, for Niki and everyone at Victor's 1959 Café thriving on the South Minneapolis corner of Thirty-Eighth and Grand

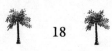

CAFÉ DE SABADO

Cozy kitchen café.
Comfort food
    in soothing ambiance.

Northwoods log
    atmosphere,
    aromas influenced
            well beyond
The American sector.

Café de Sabado:
    omelettes to order,
    bacon and eggs,
    pancakes and syrup,
            maple.
And sweet.

Fueled by Karl's
    fresh roasted
    Northland Coffee.

—May 2008 for Norma and our cozy Saturday breakfasts enjoyed together at home

CHILDHOOD INNOCENCE

"The Bolivians
    are having a party"—
    just down the block.

In a quiet neighborhood
    in Wisconsin,
    of all places!
An authentic expression
    of diversity
    growing among people
            in patterns of connection,
                    of caring.

A gathering of family
    and friends.
A coming together
    as the world
    comes apart—
    split along tattered seams
            of suspicion
                    and fear.

"The Bolivians
    are having a party"—
    so said the little boy.

In a sweet childhood innocence
    with natural humor,
    and not a hint
            of prejudice.

—February 2007 so said grandson Wesley at his house in Madison

 21

WONDERFUL WORLD

Weary.
Waiting patiently
    in old airport
        Managua.

An African.
And a *gringo*.

Embracing warmly
    in a room crowded
    with Latin Americans.

World.
Wonderful.

—May 2001 while waiting at the airport in Managua, Nicaragua, with old friend
Angetile Musomba from Tanzania

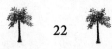

TRAIN TO SIQUERRES

On the jungle train
    narrow gauge to Siquerres—
    I unknowingly encountered
        the timeless spirit
        of Jose Figuerres.
Don Pepe
    as dynamic leader,
    as historical character
        dating to my birth
            year—1948.

With chickens and children,
    campesinos traveling
    through the countryside
        and onward
        to a new day.

The bold vision of Jose Figuerres
    points ever forward—
    to more than social progress:
        No army.
        No war.
        No weapons.
Don Pepe
    as man of peace,
    man of justice
        shining like a rainbow
        of hope.

—February 1988 on first of many trips to Costa Rica

TEN PERCENT CUT

First journey to Costa Rica
    back before *touristas*
    and eco-adventurers
        exploring tropical paradise.
Not many *gringos*
    roaming through passageways,
        narrow and confusing,
        at Mercado central.

Downtown San Jose—
    bustling with activity,
    stirring awake
        to overwhelming odors
        of fresh roasting
            coffee beans.
Picked along rugged hillsides
    as ripe,
    red cherries,
    dried and transported
        to the capital city.

Café Costa Rica
    roasterie
    for *ticos* only—
        ten-percent cut
        with coarse grain
            cane sugar.

—July 2007 thinking back to coffee inequities first learned in Costa Rica

CAFÉ BRITT

Export reserve.
Excellante beans
    grown on mountain
    hillsides chilly
        in climate *perfecto*.

Tropical plantation.
Café de Costa Rica—
    finest arabaca
    for shipping north.

Not for *ticos*
    down in the city,
    existing on inferior beans
    dumped in Mercado
        roasters.

And sold cheaper
    than dirt.

—September 2007 from Britt plantation tour in the Central Valley hillsides of Costa Rica

NORTHLAND COFFEE

Northland.
Specialty coffees
        roasted fresh
        by Karl—

In small batches,
In a small town.
In Minnesota.

Blending full-bodied
        flavors—
                carefully,
                expertly,
                personally.
Brightening wastelands
        of bland beans
        with java joy
                and misty hope.
Blazing new taste
        sensations—
                brilliantly,
                creatively,
                passionately.

Perk up—
        with Northland coffee!

—August 2007 for friend Karl in the beginning of new adventures in coffeeland

BEYOND BELIEF

Too blooming good
    to fancy
    as true.

Beyond belief.
Too chock full
    of taste,
    of real flavor
To be decaf!

Flushed free—
    no chemicals,
    no poison,
    no drugs,
    no caffeine.

In a clean water
    pure process.
Ready for roasting
    to a full-bodied
       splendor.

Too extraordinary
    to be believed
       as decaf.

—August 2007 in celebration of Karl's special Northland Coffee decaf

NORTH RUN

North run.
Distance no longer
        measured in miles
            nor time—
But in coffee stops.
Fuel for the journey.
Caffeine tripping
        all the way north
            to Ely.

Sacred Grounds
        at Stacy—
        a buzz with spirit
            and mellow music,
        cranberry scones,
            café au lait
            french roast boost.
Warming House
        at Cloquet—
        a wise motto
            for perking up:
"sit long, talk much"
        with drinks,
            coffee and cream.
Front Porch
        at Ely—
        a cozy corner
            serene atmosphere,
        hanging around music
            for coffee time
            warm welcome.

To the end of the road.
North run
        on more than empty.

—September 2007, reflections on our road trips from the Twin Cities to Ely
hopscotching coffee shops

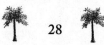

28

LEMON WOLF

Cozy cafe.
North Shore
    ambiance,
    amidst
        mammals.

Hanging around
    in carved glory—
        beaver bay,
        lemon wolf,
        laughing moose.

All welcomed warmly
    by smiling bears
    on the porch
        and among tables.

Everywhere
    but on the menu!

—April 2007 Lake Superior north shore café at Beaver Bay

PETE'S FLEET

Sitting side by side
    on the little dock
    at Chetek Bay.
Surrounded by Pete's fleet—
    an odd collection
    of boats and kayaks
        more than fitting
        for a sailor friend
           of old.

Memories linger
    of Navy times together
        on the *Observer*
        long passed away,
    of the old camp
        across the bay
        where faith formed
           and friendships
           flourished.

And in this nearby
    peaceful summer time—
        young voices dance
           on the water,
        campfire flames flicker
           in gathering darkness

As simple joys swirl
    through old memories
    and renewed connections
        with ole Pete.

—June 1994 for old Navy buddy and longtime friend Steve Peterson

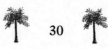

30

OLIVES AFTER ALL

Mona Lisa's
    smiling face
    familiar on Water Street.

A campus town surprise,
    in sleek modernity
        blending seamlessly
        with classy artistry.

In a down-to-earth atmosphere.
And imaginative cuisine:
    marinated Italian olives,
    feta fresh Greek salad,
    steamed Mediterranean calamari,
        and staff of life—
            comfort bread.

In soothing simplicity.
Accompanying longtime
    friendship connections
        and free ranging,
        rambling conversations.

All transcending
    time and place,
        and even Mona Lisa's
        eternally smiling
            face.

—May 2006 with friend Pete in Eau Claire

BOOKEND BUDDIES

Bookends.
Bethlehem
    downtown
    early mornings
        and late evenings
        slipping away.
Swiftly.
With bagels and beer,
    bishops abuzz.

Westerners exploring an eastern
    place of the heart,
    growing in knowing
        and being known,
        in appreciating.
And being appreciated.
Buddies
    connecting in talk
    and listening
        from dawn to dusk.

And all spaces between.
Bethlehem.
Bookends.

—October 2002 for Canadian friend Graham in celebration of our wandering
times out east

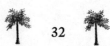

32

GUMBO GUYS

Food and foolishness
    mingle together
    in haphazard connections—

Converging.
Like baseball
    and hot dogs,
    or brats and beer.

Like close friends
    and traveling companions,
    or Velvet Soul
        and Mocha Monkey
        atmosphere.
Like gumbo
    and alligator
    and Trappey's hot sauce
        in a spicy synergy
        of friendship.

Gumbo guys.
Foolishness
    in delicious disguise,
    in culinary ties
        that bind.

—July 2007 for poetry reading opening piece, and for gumbo guys Tom, Bob, and Brian

33

ROCK HUNTERS

Rock hunters
    at Spring Hill farm.

Together.
In search of treasures
    and geology delights—
    gathered from fields of gold
    scattered among massive
        piles of debris.

Rock hunters
    at Cold Spring brewery.

Together.
In search of libations
    and chemistry insights—
    porter and bock
    a distinctive brewing
        combo delight.

Moonlight ale—
    black and tan,
    brightening darkness
        in refreshing reflections.

Rock hunters.
Together on tour—
    a limited edition
        expedition.

—April 2008 for Tom in memory of a very interesting day shared together at farm and brewery in central Minnesota

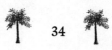

PATHWAYS

Pathways.
Paved with stones
    rugged,
      ragged and rustic.

Glistening in morning
    dew,
      peaceful and calm.

Glowing in afternoon
    sun,
      bright and inviting.

Shining—

On precious pathways
    of happiness.

Lined with generosity.

—May 2008 word play with stones and weather

POISON TRUCK

Poison truck
  rolling along suburban
        avenues.

Quietly.
Discreetly.
Disasterously
  promoting lushness
  without consequences
        naturally.

Chemicals
  invading the earth,
  polluting the air,
  infiltrating water systems
        everywhere.

Insidiously.
Incredibly shortsighted.

Poison truck
  well accepted
  without thought
        or alarm.

—July 2008 from the home front neighborhood scene

DANDELION GOLD

Golden field
    of dandelions—

Gleaming in the glory
    of May sunshine
    in the north country.
Stretching deep
    and dangerous
    across the front yard
        at Timmer Huset.

Blooming beautiful
    in full view
    of the neighbors—
        nervous.
Dreading disruption
    of artificial perfection,
    of chemically induced
        lushness.

Dandelion gold—
    an alternative definition
    of flower.

—May 2007 from the front yard at Timmer Huset

TIGER LILY

Tiger lily
>> glowing
>> in brilliant
>>>> afternoon sunshine,
>> golden treasure
>>>> of simple beauty.

Burnt orange
>> roaring
>>>> in splendor,
>> renewed message
>>>> of faith flying.

In the wary face
>> of freedom fleeing.

Tiger lily
>> casting shadows
>> in twilight
>>>> dimming.

—July 2006 while wandering around at the Minnesota Landscape Arboretum

38

ALONG THE FREEWAY

Llamas
Along the freeway
 gawking,
  mangy,
      hanging around
      in the median.
A strange sight.

Black River Crossing—
 not the highlands
      of Peru,
 not the pastures
      of Freedom,
 not the petting zoo
      of Woolrich.

Winter in Wisconsin.
Llamas along the freeway
 grazing.

—February 2003 while on the road in Wisconsin near Black River Falls

39

TRUTH WAITS

Where truth unravels.
Only for hearts
  wounded,
    tumbling into darkness
        and light,
    into confusion
        and clarity.

In places of mystery
  beneath loss of hopes,
        and dreams
        lurking.
Where truth lingers.
Only for moments
  slipping away,
  ever so quickly
        and quietly.

Where truth waits.
Only for eyes
  opening to light
        and darkness,
  to burden
        and blessing.

In places of mystery
  beyond abandonment
        and tiny shreds
        of contentment.

—July 2007 reflections on honesty

40

CHARLIE'S CAFÉ

Downtown.
Lake Wobegone.

Foggy Minnesota morning
   at Charlie's Café—
   where food nurtures
       more than bodies,
   where the people
       are the real stars.

Classic country breakfast—
   farm-fresh eggs,
   thick-cut smoked bacon,
   real fried potatoes,
   homemade wheat toast
       and butter,
         full-fat style.
Worthy of myth
   and legend.

A poet's place.
A storyteller's dream.

—July 2007 local sub-culture at Freeport along   I-94 corridor between
Minneapolis and Fargo

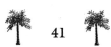

BRAT FEST

At sixty.
Mad City memories.

Tumbling back through times
   long gone
   in a murky haze.
Swirling among the throngs
   and thousands gathered
   on Willow Island.

For Brat Fest.

Grandchildren wandering
   in new memories
       unfolding.
Lurking along edges
   of all the years
       slipping away.

Through people
   and places
       of the heart.

—May 2008 only in Madison

ON THE PLATFORM

On the platform with grandpa.
Little hands stuffed
　　into pants pockets.

Warding off a morning chill.
Waiting for his railroad reality
　　to roll into the station.
Wondering about hissing steam
　　and thunder pounding
　　　　on the rails.

Suddenly—
　　the "400" appears round
　　the Washington Street bend,
　　　　majestically,
　　　　powerfully,
　　　　magically,
　　transforming calm
　　　　into bustling activity.
Screeching in on a long
　　slow motion,
　　awesome approach
　　　　to the platform audience.

Long gone now—
　　like grandpa,
　　　　like even dad—
All that remains
　　are lingering,
　　vague scenes
　　　　and vivid sounds.
And meaningful memories
　　of a little boy
　　and an old man
　　　　on the platform.

—May 2006 at least fifty years after being on the platform with Grandpa
Christianson in Green Bay

CHANNING OUTHOUSE

On the old railroad run
    past Iron Mountain
    and Sagola.
All the way to Republic.
And cabin culture—
    Lawrence style.

A quick stop in Channing
    for visiting the relatives
    and great aunt Judith's
        "little lunch"—
Never a small spread.
Never a short stop.
Never painless for city children
    encountering great uncle Carl's
        outhouse.

A slightly vented
    one-hole shack
    held together by rotting boards
        and a tiny hook
        on the flimsy door.
To keep out the bears
    and wolves of our young
        imaginations,
    and the pine snakes
        crawling around
        in our nightmares.

And through the laughter
    of old character Carl
    sending us kids out back
        with a hearty:
        "watch out boys!"

—June 2006 memories of Upper Michigan relatives Carl and Judith at the tiny village of Channing

TRUNK FULL

Torture in blackberry
        brambles
            near Chute Pond—
Picking tiny berries
        in the sunshine
        of tangled wild
                woods.

Our old '56 Oldsmobile
        parked along dusty
                roadsides—
Awaiting a bonanza
        of juicy berries
        ripe and ready
                for picking.

Keep on picking—
No stopping without
        a trunk full,
                and overflowing.
Into the massive
        back seat.

—June 2006 picking blackberries as a child in the northern Wisconsin woods
with my mother and grandmother

 45

RIB RIVER BALLROOM

Hear the old blues sax
    moaning in willows,
    weeping down stream
        around the bend
        and back through time.

At Rib River Ballroom.
Big Band echoes
    evoke faded images
    of dancing girls
        and dashing guys
        from a long gone
            era.

Gypsy queens.
Soul swooners.
Rock and Roll vibes
    all swirl in the current
    of turbulent times,
        mixing with dreams
            innocent.
And carefully disguised
    as new dreams
    of a new reality.

Hippies and Beats.
Farm boys and fair girls
    past and present
    merge at Rib River Ballroom
        in a dynamic vision
        of a future
            yet to be.

—January 2004 an old jute joint on Highway 29 near Wausau, Wisconsin

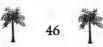

46

FOR THE BYRDS

All along Storgata
   people moved to the beat—
"Mr. Tambourine Man"
      transcending language
      and human experience.

From the Sunset Strip
   to Lillehammer street fair.
From the Hollywood Bowl
   to round the world—
"Mr. Tambourine Man"
      transforming four decades
      into simple moments
      of common recognition
        and meaning.

Here in Norway.
There in America.
And everywhere
   for the Byrds.

—January 2003 at the Lillehammer street fair late on a light summer evening in Norway at 61 degrees north latitude

47

MIRAGE

Mirage.
Marinated in time
     passing,
     fading away
          in a flash.

Like mist
     on morning breezes,
     or greek olives
          in wilderness style.
Marinated with care
     using time honored
          recipe.

From Kiki
     at Bill's Imported
          Foods.
More than mirage
     on Lake Street.

—September 2008 happy hour camping with Tom at Lake Four in the Boundary Waters Canoe Area

THUNDER BARRAGE

Thunder barrage.
Storm building slowly
        on warm air
                currents.

Floating across beautiful
        northern sky
                like a flotilla
                of ships.

Darkening clouds billowing.
Flashing streaks of lightening
        from afar,
                and closing fast
                in a wild wind.

Hail bombardment
                pounding with fury,
                pelting nylon tents
                        in surprise assault.
Giving way quickly
                to pouring rain
                        and booming thunder.
Passing through in long
                deep rumbles,
                and moving on
                        in thunder barrage.

All across border country.

—September 2008 camping with Tom in a wild storm at Lake Four

INTRUDERS

Attacked.
As intruders
   in the wilderness
   invading foreign
      terrain.

For personal gain.
Like conquistadores.
Like clueless missionaries
   and greedy merchants
   of wild fur trade
      days of old.
Of penetrating exploration
   and relentless exploitation
   of living creatures
      and evolving creation.
Like all pirates
   only passing through
      the north country.

Attacked.
As interlopers
   by swarming hordes
      of mosquitoes.
Buzzing sensitive heads.
Biting exposed flesh.
Bombing kamikaze style.
Bugging all campers
   and canoe paddlers
   not really belonging
      on their turf.

—July 2008 camping with Norma and the mosquitoes at Lake Three in the Boundary Waters

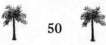

50

CROP OF ROCKS

Enemies.

Rise from the earth—
    relentlessly,
    effortlessly,
    without fail.

A perennial crop
    of rocks
    of all sizes
    and shapes.
Planted eons ago
    by glaciers
    scalping the land.
Cultivated annually
    by changing seasons
    of frost and warmth.
Harvested continuously
    by human hands
    and hauled off
    by wagon load.

Piled together.
Resting for eternity.
Waiting to be redefined
    as treasures,
    and carried away.

—May 2008 for Lou at Spring Hill farm in gratitude for all the rocks

 51

IN PERIL

For those in peril
      on landscapes
      lurking within hearts

Unfolding.
Unburdening on seas
      restless,
      reckless,
      rolling along beneath
          surface.

Realities rising.
Responsibilities
      in peril
      sinking deep into
          spirits.

Soaring.
Lifting on breezes
      gentle,
      gliding
          and soothing.

—August 2008 while working on culture change in elder-care settings

ON COFFEE AND CHOCOLATE

Coffee—
Fast forward
    speeding transmitters and thoughts,
    improving reactions and mental functions,
        boosting dopamine levels
        and enhancing moods.
Caffeine.
Drug of choice
    energizing turbo chemicals,
    promoting feelings of wakefulness
        and alertness,
        of assertiveness and aggressiveness.
In excess.
Regress to heightened activity.

Chocolate—
Brown gold
    bringing passion and nutrition,
    creating allure and fashion,
        cultivating romance
        and stirring emotions.
Calories.
Treat of choice
    engaging delicate style,
    provoking feelings of elegance
        and simplicity,
        of sweetness and bitterness.
In regress.
Excess of deepened stimulation.

Together.
Coffee and chocolate –
    more than caffeine and calories.
Combining together in dynamic synergy,
    in a sensual jolt.

—March 2008 while relaxing with Norma at Cove Point Lodge on Lake Superior

OLD VICTORIA

Old Victoria
    shudders awake
    from long slumber
        decaying,
        denying changing times.

Coming alive.
Renewing heart
    and hope
    in creating atmosphere.
Uplifting.
Upbeat.
Stimulating.
Bringing people together
    with healthy food
    and interesting drinks
        and music.

In dramatic transformation
    from Tuffy's old,
    dilapidated tavern
        to School of the Wise.
More than a long trip
    from nowhere.

—July 2007 on site downtown Victoria at the School of the Wise

FLOYD'S

Caribbean corner
    carefree atmosphere
    livening up
        nights.

Lights sparkling.
Traveled Ground band
    rocking the porch
    way out back
        at Floyd's.

Formerly Leo's Bar—
    cozy tavern hangout
    on catholic corner.
Caribbean vibes
    transforming old Victoria
    with red stripe
        and reggae.

Music.
Fake palm trees.
Pirates lurking
    on rooftops sagging
    under fresh burdens
        of glory.
Princes drinking
    despair away,
    and princesses dancing
        in abandon.

—June 2008 relaxing Caribbean style at 42 degrees north latitude

ROOTS BAND

Traveling ground
    through fertile soil
        of roots music.

American style—
    blending blues and folk,
        rockabilly and country,
           and rock 'n' roll
    into heartfelt expressions
        woven into the soul
        of humanity.

Down to earth.
Real and more real.
Keep on traveling ground
    through soaring horizons
        of humanity—

Bright with promise
    and possibility.

—June 2007 for Clark and the band

MIGHTY PEC

Early March.
Danger flowing fast
      on icy waters
         of spring thawing,
            melting,
            arriving.

Southern Wisconsin style.
All along the mighty
      Pecatonica River.
Argyle town.
Awaiting
      foolish paddlers
      in search of thrills
         and disaster.

Shooting the damn
      on purpose
      in a capsizing flurry
         of stupidity.

—March 2008 all these thirty-five years after near disaster paddling the folbot
over a dam on the Pecatonica River

 57

HATTERAS RECALLED

East Carolina lowlands.
Scrub pine
    and flower farms.
Hay pastures
    and tobacco barns
    ramshackle with time gone by,
        well worn with wind
           and water.

Hints of old cotton fields
    appear in tattered disarray
      of long ago
        low country.
Sand dunes
    and brackish inlets.
Soaring sea gulls
    and Albemarle Sound
    sparkling in the morning sun
      all the way
        to outer banks.

Outer Banks
    from inside passage
    more than three decades
      past Cape Hatteras
      turmoil.
Inside calm
    from challenges
    and changes
      coming on a new
        horizon.

—April 2006 while visiting my brother Steve on the Outer Banks at Nag's Head

AKUMAL

Mayan rabbit
  running across full moon,
  reflecting bright
      on water sparkling
      at Half Moon Bay.

Paradise found
  in pristine beaches
      of white sand purity.
Paradise disrupted
  in armed soldiers
      of beach drug patrol.

Akumal—
  Place of the Turtle
      on Riviera Maya.

La Joya—
  Jewel of the Yucatan.

Relaxation the Caribbean way.
Life in the slow lane
  where time moves
  like the sea
      and the turtles—

Relentlessly
Crawling slower than motion,
  moving along with waves
      and surf.
Time—
  slipping away
  in rhythms gentle
      and free.

—July 2004 while at Akumal with Norma, and friends Carol and Larry

RUNDOWN

Rundown—
Nica food
   adventure.

Time travel—
   from Barra del Colorado
      veranda fish,
      on a steamy
         tropical night
   to Palo Alto
      fellowship,
      and new friends
         in California.

Running it down
   in sweet milk
   of young coconut:
      cassava,
      banana,
      vegetables,
      mystery meat.

Anything you can
   run down
   in the jungle
      and cook
         in a pot.

—July 2004 for Captain Jack Kandler with fond memories of my first rundown experience, and all the Nica friends I've eaten rundown with over the years

LONG WAY

Long way
    from Dar es Salaam—
        dusty,
        dirty,
        downtrodden.

Pathways
    of hearts united
    in common experiences
    of work,
        worship,
            and wonder.

Afar.
Around the world
    and near at home—
        Dunn Brothers
        Coffee.

In downtown
    Chaska.

—July 2008 while walking in downtown Chaska on the way to meeting a former colleague from afar

61

HEARTS WARMING

Third World
Reflections
  from a first world
      person.

On hearts
  wrenching,
  warming in many movements
      between sorrow
        and gladness.

In moments
  diminishing,
  dashing hopes of humanity
      upon rocks
        of suffering.

With minds
  boggling,
  stretching toward horizons
      teeming with dreams
        and visions.

Fresh.
And always new.

—May 2007 reflections on third world experiences and memories

ORIGINAL COLORS

Birthmarks.
Splattered on the canvas
    of humanity—
        randomly.
Tattered with familiarity.

Colors of origin.
Stretching back through time
    to fields of blue
    and bays of green:
        de colores
        azul e verde.

Like dear friends
    transcending differences
    of culture and geography
        and race:
        de colores
        negro e blanco.

White and black.
Merging in strands of identity
    and original colors:
        Green Bay.
        Bluefields.
Connected together
    in an often used,
    yet simple prayer:

"For health and strength
    and daily food,
    we give you thanks,
        O Lord."

—March 2007 with me and Oliver firmly in mind

 63

ENOUGH IS ENOUGH

Neighborhood
Named enough—
   on the boundary
      of reclaiming
Time.
Taking back gifts and graces.
With a sense of retreat
   as celebrating moment
      to moment.
Honoring spirit.
Marking days of rest
   and embracing leisure
   without guilt or shame.
In a not enough world:
   not enough time nor space,
   not enough play nor rest,
   not enough heart nor soul energy.
In a vitality deprived,
   work obsessed culture.
Fast and frantic.
Rushed and harried.
Enough never being enough
   in the neighborhood
   on the near side of clutter.
And confusion yearning for clarity.
With a rhythm of retreat
   turning heart beats slowly.
Renewing sacredness.
Restoring simplicity
   and embracing time
   with meaningful moments.
In an enough
   is finally enough world:
Connecting small steps
   on a long journey
   toward wholeness and healing.

—March 2007, reflections on slowing down and reclaiming time as moments
to enjoy and appreciate

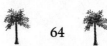

SOUTH

OF

CONTRARY

FACES OF THE HEART

South of extraordinary—

A thrilling diversity
        uniting emotional reality
                into scenes
                of mystery
                        and wonder.

West of everywhere—

An expansive vision
        seeing faces of the heart
                as journeys
                of contented
                        beauty.

—November 2008 with hints of another book of poetry coming

OMBRE

Shades blending,
    fading gradually
    from light hue
        to dark.

Ombre—
Fabric colors colliding
    in fuzzy patterns
        of creativity.
And vibrancy
    dancing through shadows
    deepening in gloomy
        joy.

And ambiguity.
Like foul-weather clothes
    clinging to attitudes
    brightening in sunny
        despair.

Along with stark wisdom
    from an old,
        time worn
Proverb from Norway:
    "No bad weather.
    Just bad clothes."

—March 2008 while relaxing with Norma at Cove Point Lodge on the shore of
Lake Superior

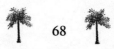

68

JAVA JUNKY

Java junky
    perking on edges
        of morning.

Jitters.
Clearing through foggy
    beginnings,
    slipping along ledges
        of confusion.
On the funky way
    to clarity,
    to monkey business.

Swirling through vibrations
    of connection
        and friendship,
    of reflection
        and renewal.

Java junky
    perking all day
        into evening.

—April 2008 for Pam and Mark and the whole Mocha Monkey crew

LAKE THREE CHURCH

Sunday morning vacation.
Skipping church
       spectacular
       at Lake Three
              Church.

In the pines.
High Camp vistas
       of creation beauty
              and splendor.

In the wilds.
Choir of loons
       accompanying prayers
              of quiet solitude.
While eagles soar
       and beavers
              entertain.
And sermons sound
       in hushed voices
              of water.

Lapping on rocky
       shorelines
              gently.

—July 2008 from Sunday morning on vacation with Norma at High Camp

DEEP

Deep.
In the heart
    of lake country.

Roots of trees.
Rotting muskeg bogs.
Rocks scattered haphazardly
    in patterns born
        beyond time.

Reach of rivers.
Running from gravity
    wild and free
    on the wind.
Ruffling in big pines
    and across open
        waters.

Deep.
In the soul
    of humanity.

—April 2008 at Cove Point on the north shore

LAKE FOUR LULLABY

Harvest moon
        rising in surprise,
        orange and bright
                on distant treetops.

Darkening in autumn
        evening stillness,
                solitude.
Majestic old pines
        murmuring,
        whispering in gentle
                breezes.
Accompanied by rapids afar
        humming,
        singing in lullaby
                melody.

For weary paddlers
        sleeping
                peacefully.

—September 2008 while camped out near the end of Lake Four with Tom

72

MAKE TIME

Make time
     in slim margins
     of busyness
        and business.

As usual.
Not necessarily normal,
     and certainly not
        healthy.

Make spaces
     in precious time
     appearing between
       work
       and play.

In treasured seams
     of creativity
     and diminishing
       activity.

Make time
     in quiet moments
       of solitude.

—January 2008 reflections on balanced living

73

THROW PAINT

If—
"Life is a great
          big canvas"—
Like Danny Kaye
          boldly announced
          to the world
                    of comedy.

Then—
"You should throw
          all the paint
          on it you can"—
And more.
As the fabric of life
          comes alive—

Vibrant
Like a rainbow
          shimmering
          in the golden sun.

Throw paint.
Don't hesitate—
          a masterpiece
                    unfolding.

Before your eyes.
Within your heart.
Like a new morning
          dawning bright,
                    chock full
                    of possibility.

—February 2007 inspiration from the bathroom of the Mocha Monkey Coffee
Shop in Waconia—now resting there in a rustic frame

74

NO PERFECT ENDING

No perfect ending
        in the great mystery
        of life and death
                swirling together
                        in patterns
Imperfect.

No clarity
        in wonderful ambiguity
        of reclaiming shadows
                brooding
                        starkly.

No silence
        in lessons of darkness
                springing forth
                        in voices.

Of light.
And hope.

—May 2008 in celebration of the great cycle of life and light

HAKUNNA MATATA

Whisper on trade winds of hope.
Gentle tropical breeze blowing,
                    flowing,
                        bringing anew
        a timeless message
        shared among friends
                in voices hushed
                    and calm:
Hakunna Matata—
        a strange word,
        an odd concept
                for we who fret and stew
                        and worry too much,
                for we who are anxious,
                            uptight,
                            tense.
        Far too tense about the small
                as well as the big stuff
                    of life.
Hakunna Matata—
        a Swahili word meaning
                calm down,
                relax,
                take it easy,
                    go with the flow.
        Breaking tension
                with a hearty laugh,
                or at least the hint
                    of a smile.
        An expression unable to be uttered
                in total seriousness.
        Wisdom and wonder
                lead to calm hearts
                and peaceful spirits.
Hakunna Matata—Give it a try!

—May 2001 for Oliver Hodgson my *hakunna matata* friend while together in
Bluefields, Nicaragua

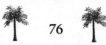

76